Impressum
Verlag: BABADADA GmbH, Nedderfeld 112 , 22529 Hamburg
Geschäftsführer / Verlagsleitung: Harald Hof
Druck: Books on Demand GmbH, In de Tarpen 42, 22848 Norderstedt

Imprint
Publisher: BABADADA GmbH, Nedderfeld 112 , 22529 Hamburg, Germany
Managing Director / Publishing direction: Harald Hof
Print: Books on Demand GmbH, In de Tarpen 42, 22848 Norderstedt

school

escola

divide
dividir

$186/2$

board
tauler

classroom
classe

school yard
pati (de l'escola)

teacher
professor

paper
paper

write
escriure

pen
estilogràfica

desk
escriptori

ruler
regle

book
llibre

pupil
estudiant

satchel

bossa

pencil case

estoig

pencil

llapis

pencil sharpener

maquineta de fer punta

rubber

goma

drawing pad

bloc de dibuix

drawing

dibuix

paintbrush

pinzell

paint box

capsa de pintures

scissors

tisores

glue

cola

exercise book

quadern d'exercicis

homework

deures

number

nombre

add

afegir

subtract

sostreure

multiply

multiplicar

calculate

calcular

letter

lletra

alphabet

alfabet

word

mot

text

text

read

llegir

chalk

guix

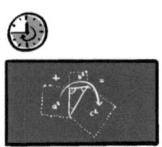

lesson

lliçó

register

llibre de classe

examination

examen

certificate

certificat

school uniform

uniforme escolar

education

formació

encyclopedia

enciclopèdia

university

universitat

microscope

microscopi

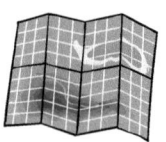

map

mapa

waste-paper basket

paperera

travel
viatge

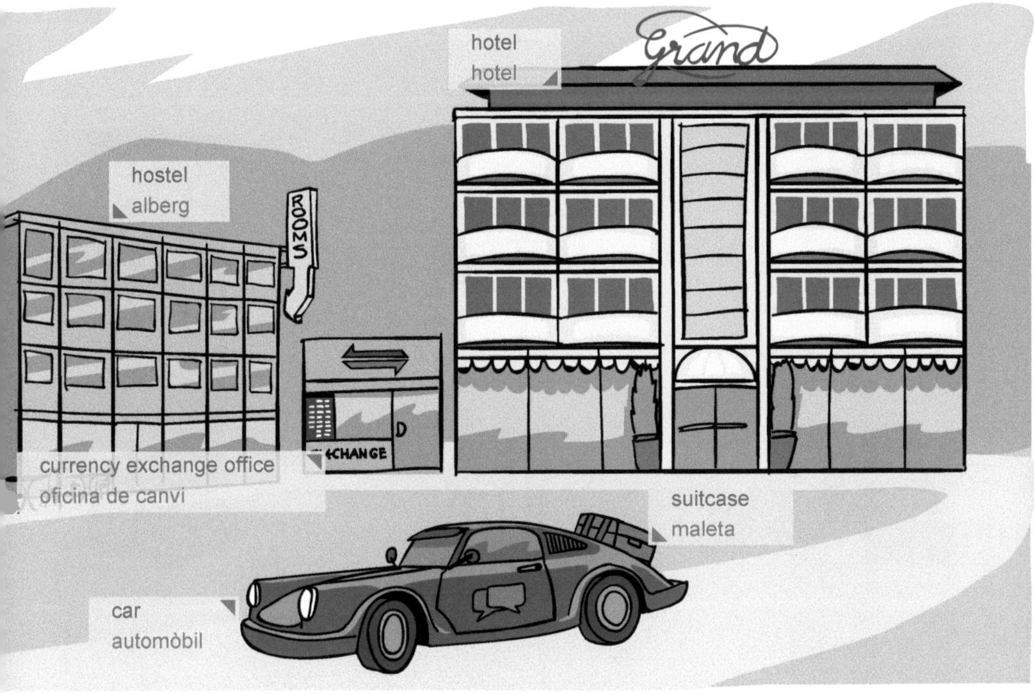

hotel
hotel
Grand
hostel
alberg
ROOMS
EXCHANGE
currency exchange office
oficina de canvi
suitcase
maleta
car
automòbil

language
llengua

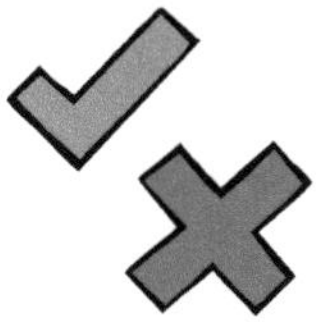

yes / no
sí / no

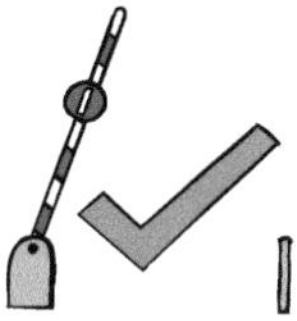

Okay
D'acord

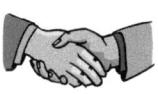

hello
Ey!

translator
traductora

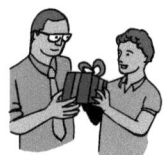

Thank you
gràcies

how much is...?

Quant costa... ?

I don´t get it

No entenc

problem

problema

Good evening!

Bona nit!

Good morning!

bon dia!

Good night!

bona nit!

goodbye

fins aviat

direction

direcció

luggage

bagatge

bag

bossa

backpack

sarrona

guest

convidat

room

cambra

sleeping bag

sac de dormir

tent

tenda

tourist information	beach	credit card
oficina de turisme	platja	carta de crèdit

breakfast	lunch	dinner
esmorzar	dinar	sopar

Ticket	elevator	stamp
bitllet	ascensor	segell

border	customs	embassy
frontera	duana	ambaixada

visa	passport	
visat	passaport	

transport
transport

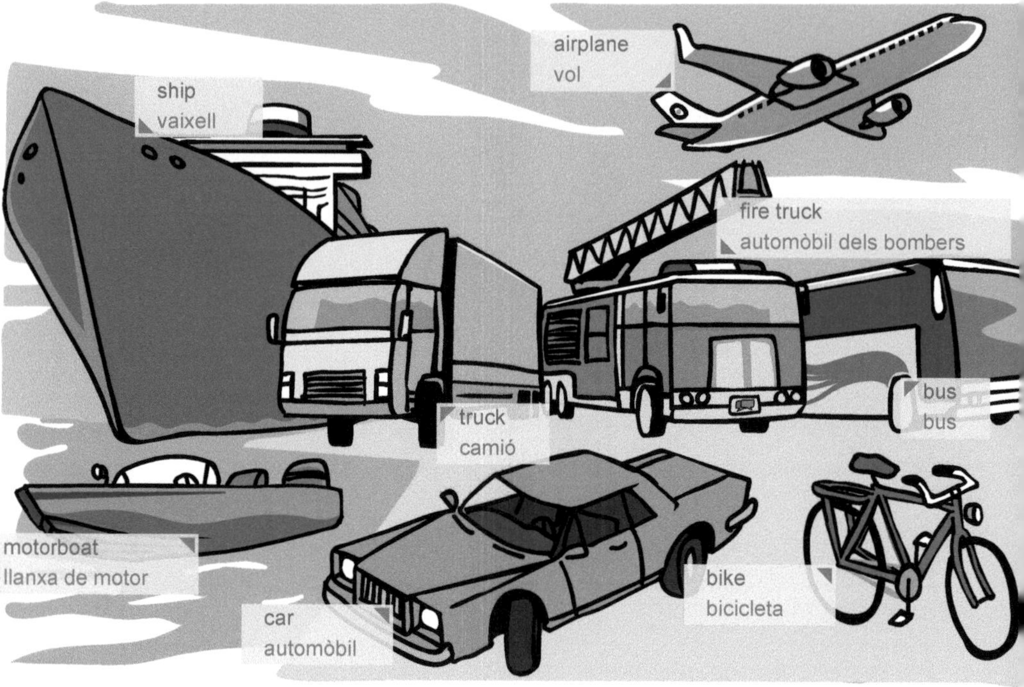
airplane
vol
ship
vaixell
fire truck
automòbil dels bombers
bus
bus
truck
camió
motorboat
llanxa de motor
bike
bicicleta
car
automòbil

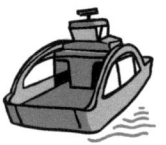

ferry

transbordador

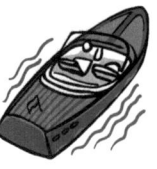

boat

barca

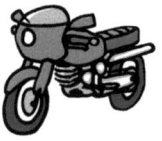

motorbike

moto

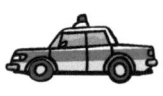

police car

automòbil de policia

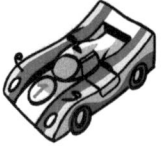

racing car

automòbil de curses

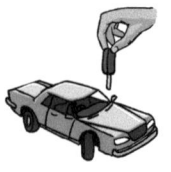

rental car

automòbil de lloguer

car sharing

vehicle compartit

tow truck

grua

garbage truck

camió de les escombraries

engine

motor

fuel

benzina

fuel station

benzineria

traffic sign

senyal de trànsit

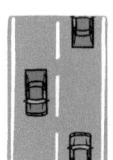

traffic

trànsit

traffic jam

embús

parking lot

aparcament

train station

estació de trens

tracks

vies

train

tren

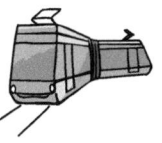

tram

tramvia

wagon

vagó

helicopter

helicòpter

airport

aeroport

tower

torre

passenger

passatger

container

contenidor

carton

capsa de cartó

cart

carretó

basket

cistella

take off / land

enlairar-se / aterrar

city

ciutat

village

poble

city center

centre de la ciutat

house

casa

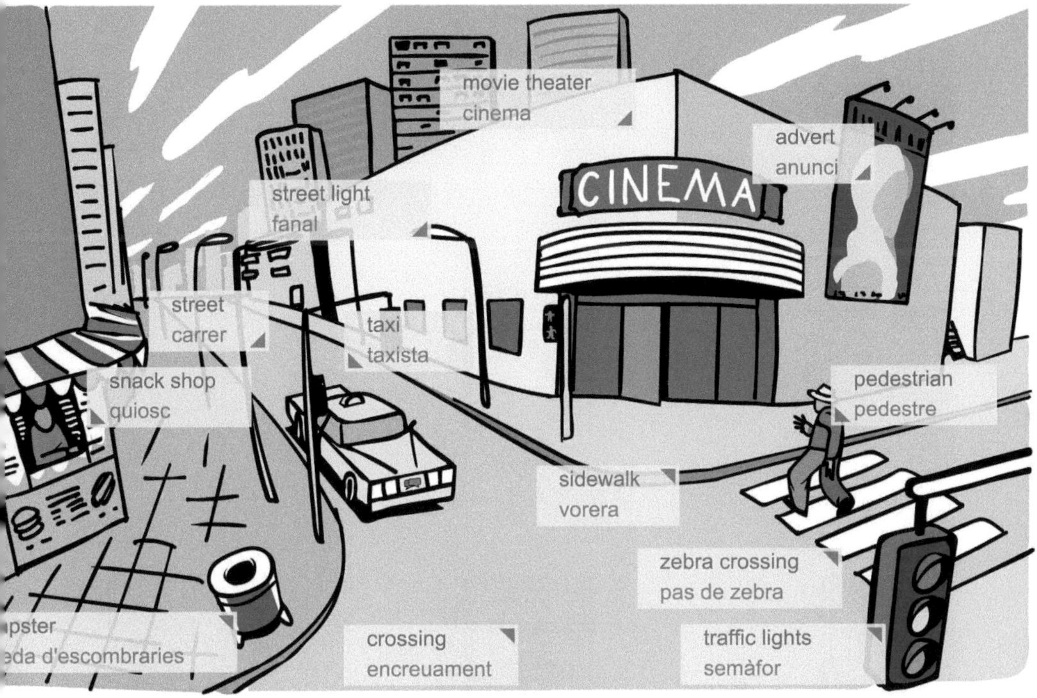

movie theater
cinema
advert
anunci
CINEMA
street light
fanal
street
carrer
taxi
taxista
snack shop
quiosc
pedestrian
pedestre
sidewalk
vorera
zebra crossing
pas de zebra
pster
eda d'escombraries
crossing
encreuament
traffic lights
semàfor

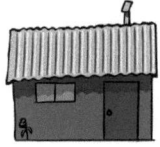

hut

cabana

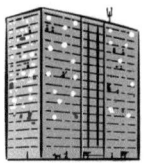

apartment

apartament

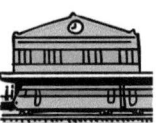

train station

estació de trens

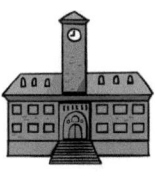

city hall

casa de la vila-ciutat

MUSEUM

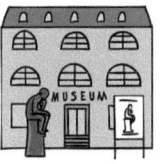

museum

museu

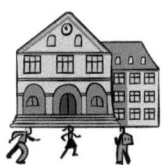

school

escola

university

universitat

bank

banca

hospital

hospital

hotel

hotel

pharmacy

farmàcia

office

oficina

book shop

llibreria

shop

botiga

flower shop

floristeria

supermarket

supermercat

market

mercat

department store

gran magatzem

fishmonger's shop

peixateria

mall

centre comercial

harbor

port

park
parc

bench
banc

bridge
pont

stairs
escala

subway
metro

tunnel
túnel

bus stop
parada d'autobús

bar
bar

restaurant
restaurant

postbox
bústia de correu

street sign
senyal indicador

parking meter
parquímetre

zoo
zoo

swimming pool
piscina

mosque
mesquita

farm

granja

pollution

pol·lució

cemetery

cementiri

church

església

playground

parc infantil

temple

temple

landscape

paisatge

leaf
fulla

signpost
cartell indicador

path
camí

meadow
prat

stone
pedra

tree
arbre

hiker
excursionista

river
riu

grass
gespa

flower
flor

valley

vall

hill

muntanya

lake

llac

forest

bosc

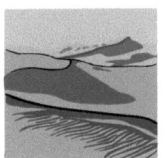

desert

desert

volcano

volcà

castle

castell

rainbow

arc de Sant Martí

mushroom

bolet

palm tree

palmera

mosquito

moscard

fly

mosca

ant

formiga

bee

abella

spider

aranya

landscape - paisatge

15

beetle

escarabat

frog

granota

squirrel

esquirol

hedgehog

eriçó

hare

llebre

owl

òliba

bird

ocell

swan

cigne

boar

senglar

deer

cervo

moose

ant

dam

presa

wind turbine

turbina

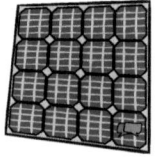

solar panel

panell solar

climate

clima

restaurant

restaurant

waiter
cambrer
menu
menú
chair
cadira
soup
sopa
pizza
pizza
cutlery
coberts
tablecloth
tovalla

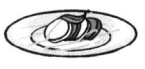

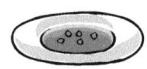

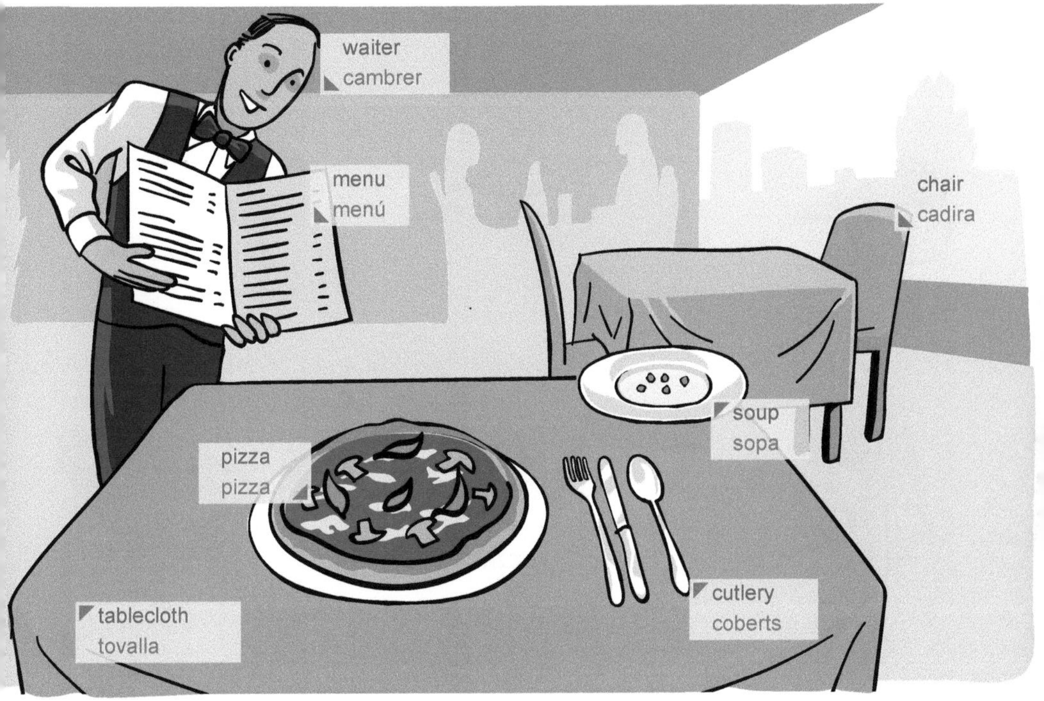

starter

primer plat

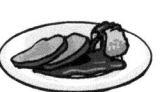

main course

plat principal

dessert

darreries

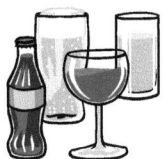

drinks

begudes

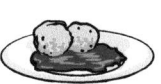

food

menjar

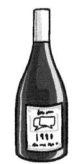

bottle

ampolla

fast food

menjar ràpid

street food

menjar de carrer

teapot

tetera

sugar bowl

sucrer

portion

porció

espresso machine

màquina d'espresso

high chair

trona

bill

factura

tray

plata

knife

ganivet

fork

forqueta

spoon

cullera

teaspoon

cullereta

serviette

tovalló

glass

got

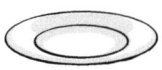

plate

plat

soup plate

plat de sopa

saucer

plateret

sauce

salsa

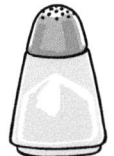

salt shaker

saler

pepper mill

molinet de pebre

vinegar

vinagre

oil

oli

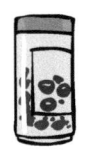

spices

espècies

ketchup

quètxup

mustard

mostassa

mayonnaise

maionesa

supermarket
supermercat

special offer
oferta especial
FOR
customer
client
dairy products
productes lactis
fruit
fruites
shopping cart
carret de la compra

BUTCHERS

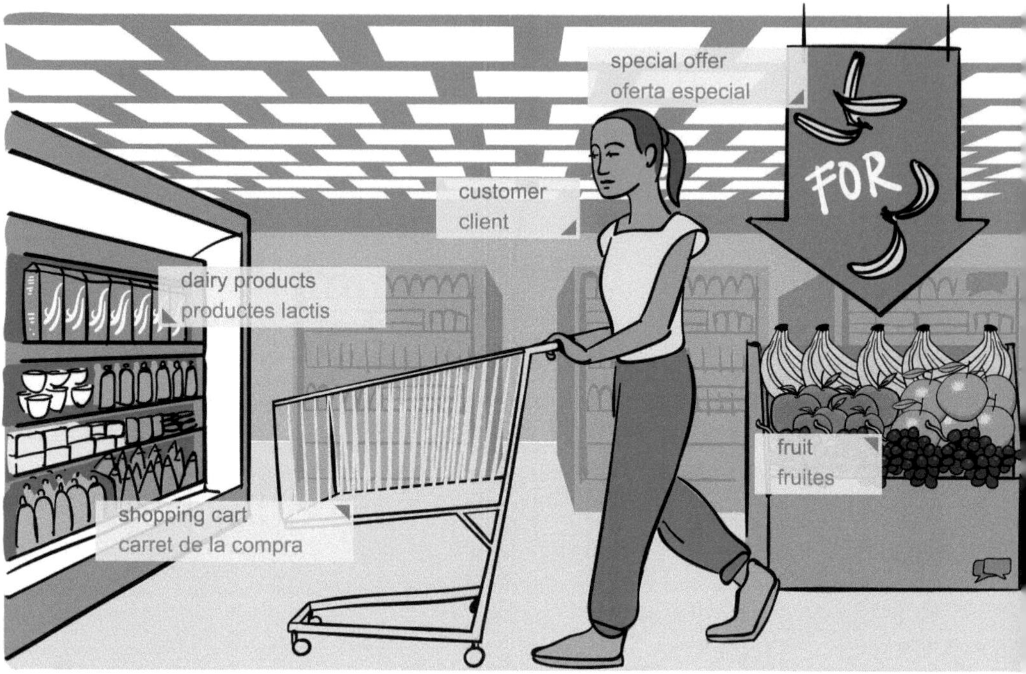

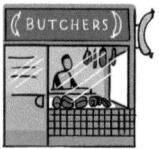

butcher's shop

carnisseria

BAKERY

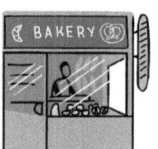

bakery

forn de pa

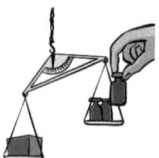

weigh

pesar

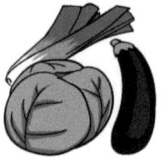

vegetables

verdures

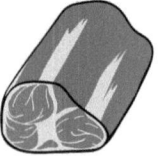

meat

carn

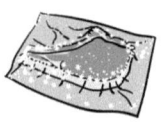

frozen food

menjar congelat

cold cuts

carn freda

canned food

conserves

detergent

detergent en pols

candy

dolços

household products

articles domèstics

cleaning products

productes de neteja

sales representative

venedora

cash register

caixa registradora

cashier

caixera

shopping list

llista de la compra

opening hours

horari d'obertura

wallet

portamonedes

credit card

carta de crèdit

bag

bossa

plastic bag

bossa de plàstic

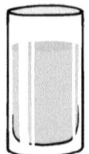

water

aigua

juice

suc

milk

llet

coke

coca-cola

wine

vi

beer

cervesa

alcohol

alcohol

cocoa

cacau

tea

te

coffee

cafè

espresso

espresso

cappuccino

cappuccino

banana

banana

apple

poma

orange

taronja

melon

síndria

lemon

llimona

carrot

pastanaga

garlic

all

bamboo

bambú

onion

ceba

mushroom

bolet

nuts

avellanes

noodles

fideus

spaghetti

espaguetis

rice

arròs

salad

amanida

fries

patates fregides

fried potatoes

patates fregides

pizza

pizza

hamburger

hamburguesa

sandwich

entrepà

escalope

escalopa

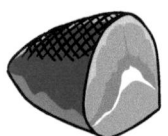

ham

cuixot

salami

salami

sausage

salsitxa

chicken

pollastre

roast

rostit

fish

peix

porridge oats

flocs de civada

muesli

musli

cornflakes

cereals

flour

farina

croissant

croissant

bread roll

panet

bread

pa

toast

torrada

cookies

bescuits

butter

mantega

curd

mató

cake

pastís

egg

ou

fried egg

ou fregit

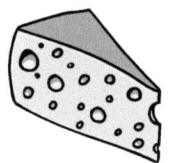

cheese

formatge

ice cream

gelat

sugar

sucre

honey

mel

jelly

melmelada

nougat cream

crema de xocolata

curry

curri

farm

granja

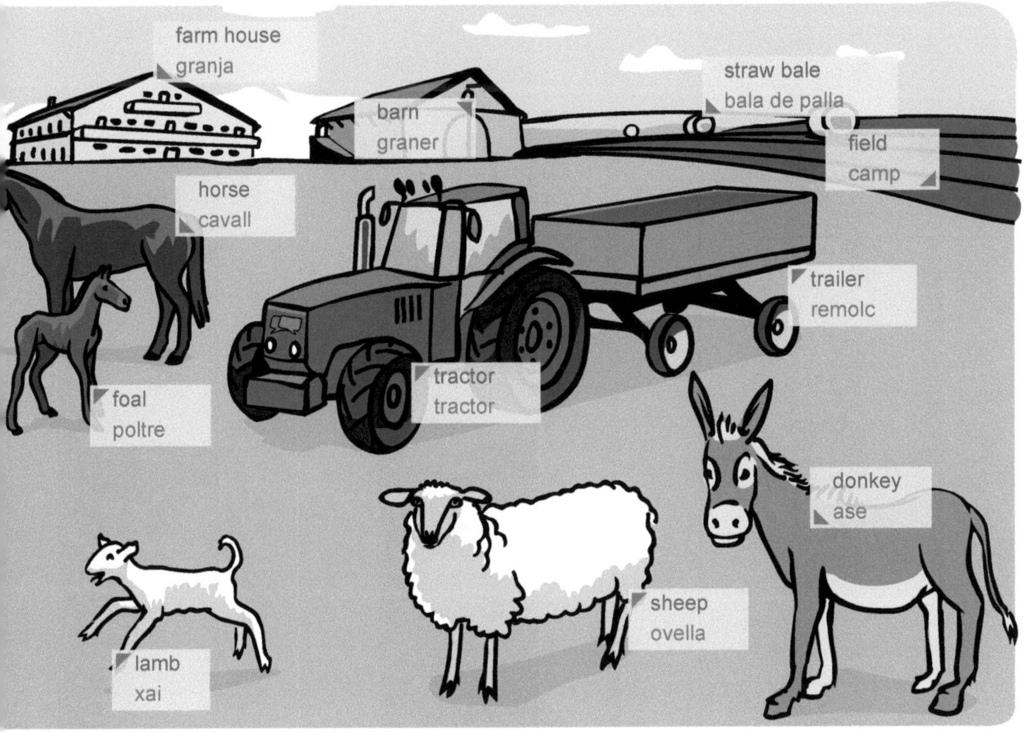

farm house
granja
straw bale
bala de palla
barn
graner
field
camp
horse
cavall
trailer
remolc
tractor
tractor
foal
poltre
donkey
ase
sheep
ovella
lamb
xai

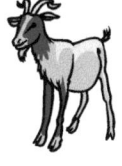

goat

cabra

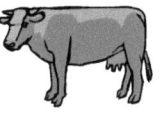

cow

vaca

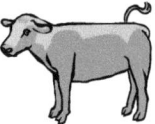

calf

vedella

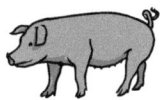

pig

porc

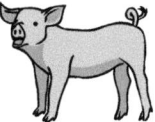

piglet

garrí

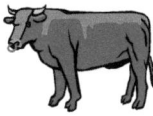

bull

bou

goose

oca

duck

ànec

chick

poll

hen

gall

cockerel

gallina

rat

rata

cat

gat

mouse

ratolí

ox

bou

dog

gos

dog house

gossera

garden hose

mànega de regar

watering can

regadora

scythe

dalla

plow

arada

sickle

falç

hoe

aixada

pitchfork

forca

axe

destral

pushcart

carretó

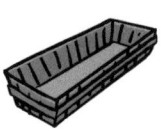

trough

abeurador

milk can

lletera

sack

sac

fence

tanca

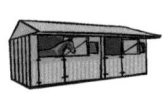

stable

establa

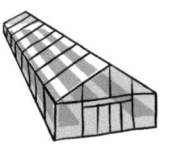

greenhouse

hivernacle

soil

sòl

seed

llavor

fertilizer

adob

combine harvester

collidora

harvest

collir

harvest

collita

yams

nyam

wheat

blat

soya

soja

potato

patata

corn

blat de moro o d'indi

rapeseed

colza

fruit tree

arbre fruiter

manioc

mandioca

grain

cereals

house
casa

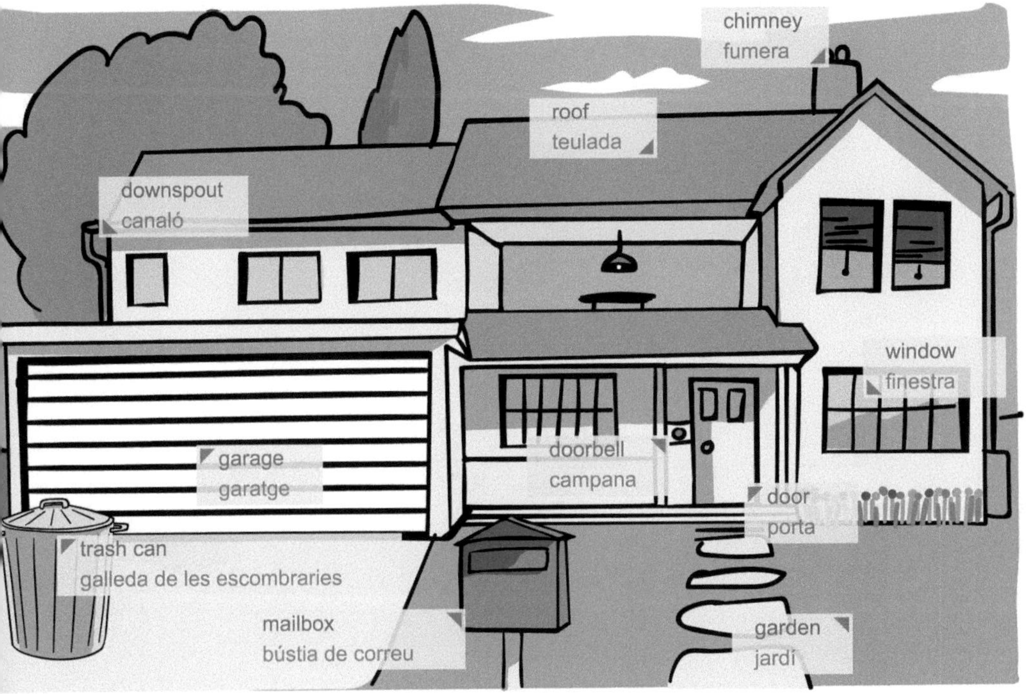
chimney
fumera
roof
teulada
downspout
canaló
window
finestra
doorbell
campana
garage
garatge
door
porta
trash can
galleda de les escombraries
mailbox
bústia de correu
garden
jardí

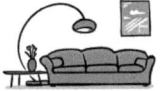

living room

sala d'estar

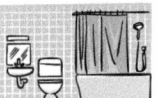

bathroom

bany

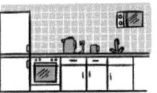

kitchen

cuina

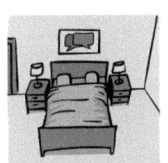

bedroom

cambra de dormir

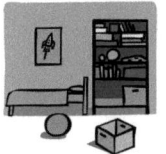

kids room

cambra de nen

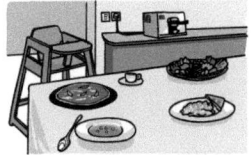

dining room

menjador

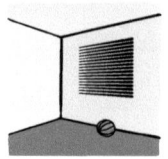

floor

sòl

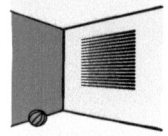

wall

paret

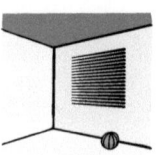

ceiling

sostre

cellar

soterrani

sauna

sauna

balcony

balcó

terrace

terrassa

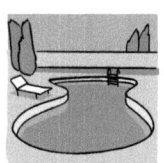

pool

piscina

lawn mower

tallagespa

sheet

vànova

bedspread

cobrellit

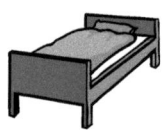

bed

llit

broom

escombra

bucket

galleda

switch

interruptor

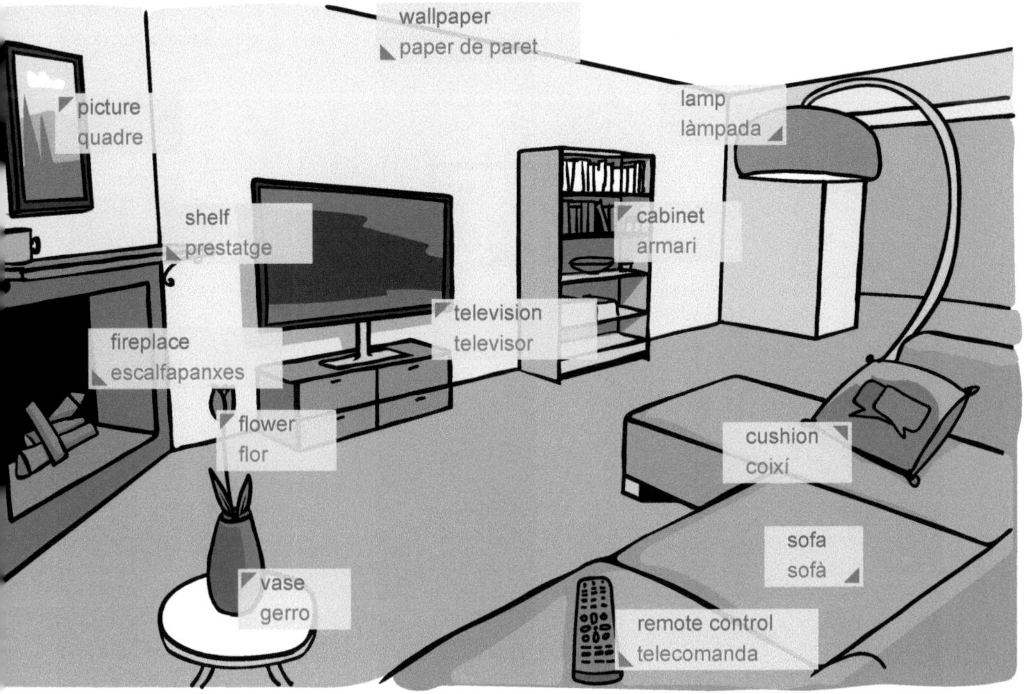

wallpaper
paper de paret

picture
quadre

lamp
làmpada

shelf
prestatge

cabinet
armari

television
televisor

fireplace
escalfapanxes

flower
flor

cushion
coixí

sofa
sofà

vase
gerro

remote control
telecomanda

carpet
catifa

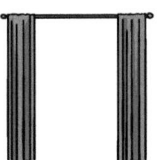

drape
cortina

table
taula

chair
cadira

rocking chair
cadira gronxadora

armchair
cadiral

book

llibre

blanket

llençol

decoration

decoració

firewood

llenya

film

film

stereo system

cadena de música

key

clau

newspaper

diari

painting

pintura

poster

cartell

radio

ràdio

notebook

bloc de notes

vacuum cleaner

aspiradora

cactus

cactus

candle

candela

kitchen
cuina

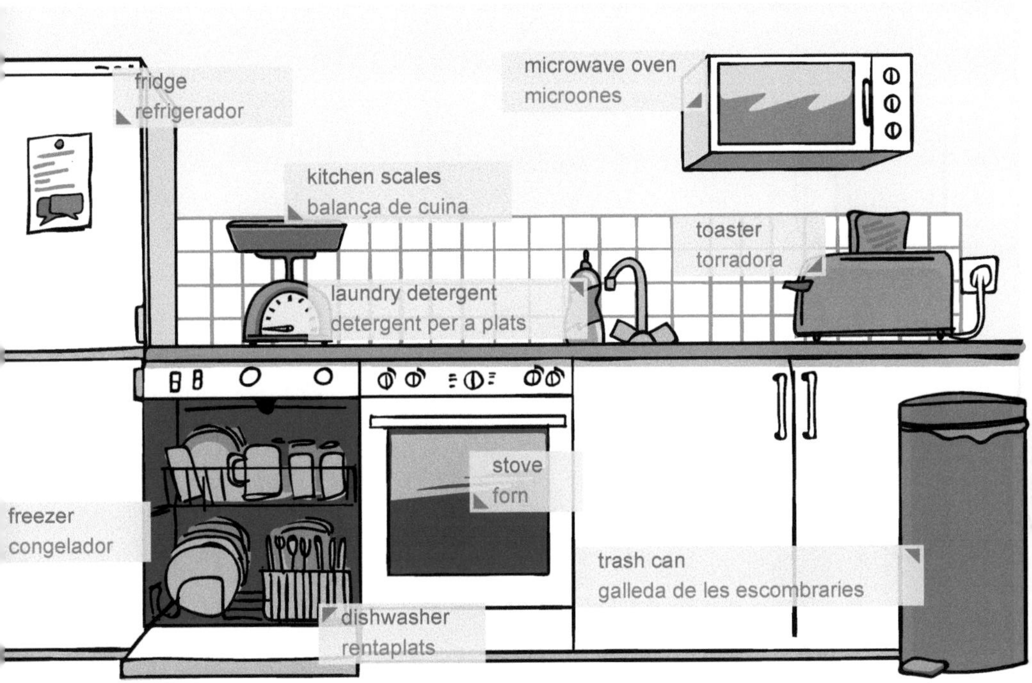

fridge
refrigerador
microwave oven
microones
kitchen scales
balança de cuina
toaster
torradora
laundry detergent
detergent per a plats
stove
forn
freezer
congelador
trash can
galleda de les escombraries
dishwasher
rentaplats

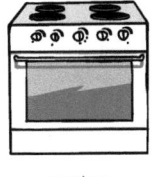

cooker

cuina de fogons

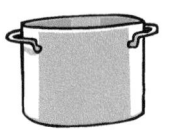

pot

olla

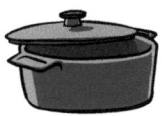

cast-iron pot

olla de ferro colat

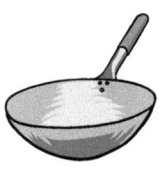

wok / kadai

wok / karahi

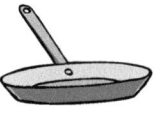

pan

paella

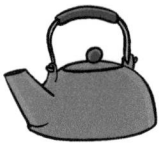

kettle

bullidor

steamer

olla de vapor

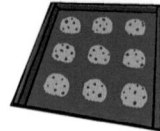

baking tray

plata de forn

crockery

vaixella

mug

tassa grossa

bowl

bol

chopsticks

bastonets xinesos

ladle

culler

spatula

espàtula

whisk

batedor

strainer

colador

sieve

sedàs

grater

ratllador

mortar

morter

barbecue

barbacoa

fireplace

foc a terra

chopping board

taula de tallar

rolling pin

corró

corkscrew

llevataps

can

pot de conserva

can opener

obridor

oven cloth

agafador

sink

aigüera

brush

raspall

sponge

esponja

blender

batedora

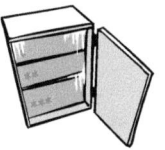

deep freezer

congelador

baby bottle

biberó

tap

aixeta

bathroom

bany

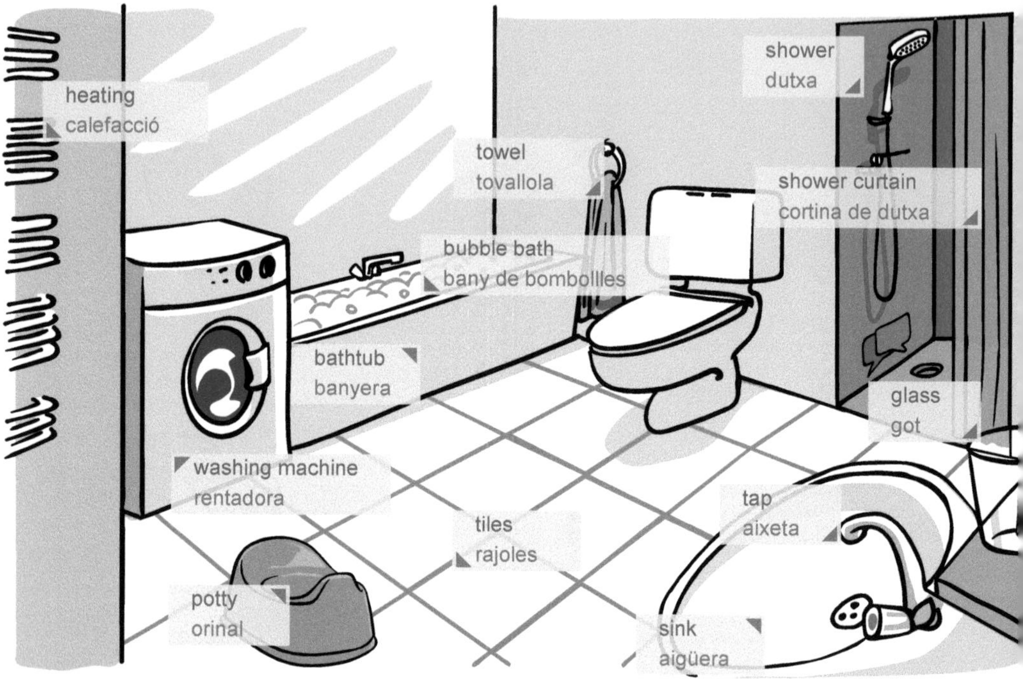
heating
calefacció
towel
tovallola
shower
dutxa
shower curtain
cortina de dutxa
bubble bath
bany de bombolles
bathtub
banyera
glass
got
washing machine
rentadora
tap
aixeta
tiles
rajoles
potty
orinal
sink
aigüera

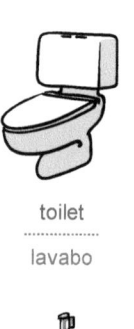

toilet

lavabo

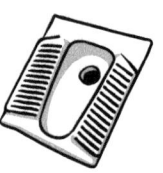

squat toilet

lavabo turc

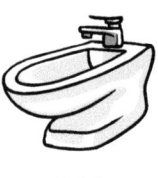

bidet

bidet

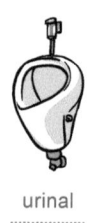

urinal

orinador

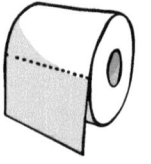

toilet paper

paper higiènic

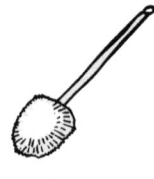

toilet brush

escombreta de sanitari

toothbrush

raspall de dents

toothpaste

pasta de dents

dental floss

fil dental

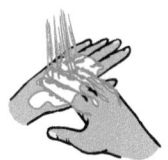

wash

rentar

hand shower

pom de dutxa

douche

dutxa íntima

basin

rentamans

back brush

raspall per a l'esquena

soap

sabó

shower gel

gel de dutxa

shampoo

xampú

flannel

manyopla de bany

drain

bonera

creme

crema

deodorant

desodorant

mirror

mirall

hand mirror

mirall-espill de mà

razor

maquineta de rasar

shaving foam

espuma de barbejar

aftershave

loció post-rasada

comb

pinta

brush

raspall

hair-dryer

eixugador

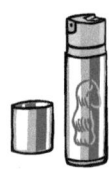

hairspray

laca

makeup

maquillatge

lipstick

pintallavis

nail varnish

esmalt d'ungles

cotton wool

cotó

nail scissors

tallaungles

perfume

perfum

washbag

estoig de bellesa

stool

tamboret

weighing scales

bàscula

bathrobe

barnús

rubber gloves

guants de goma

tampon

compresa higiènica

sanitary towel

compresa

chemical toilet

sanitari químic

kids room

cambra de nen

alarm clock
despertador
cuddly toy
animal de peluix
toy car
auto de joguina
rattle
sonall
doll's house
casa de nines
present
present

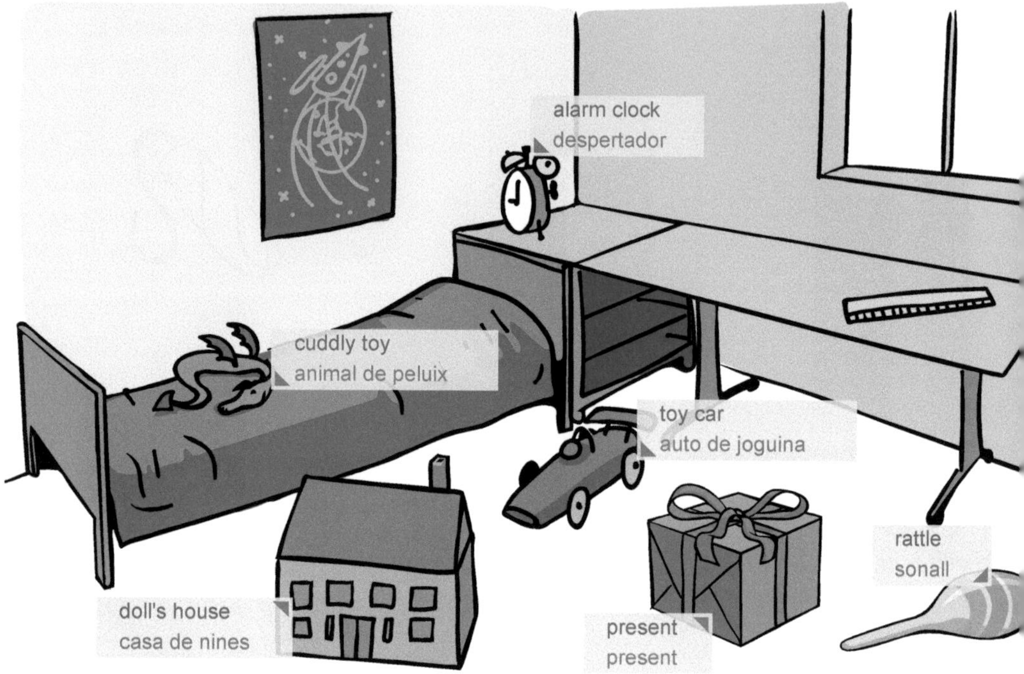

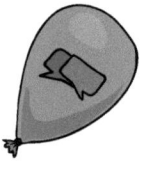

balloon

baló

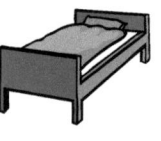

bed

llit

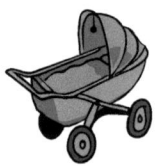

stroller

cotxet per a nens

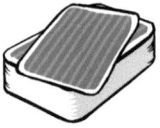

deck of cards

joc de cartes

SUPER
MEGA

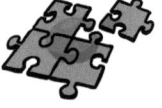

jigsaw

trencaclosca

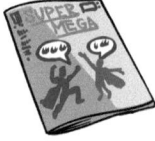

comic

historieta

lego bricks

peces de lego

toy blocks

peces de construcció

action figure

ninot d'acció

romper suit

granota

frisbee

frisbee

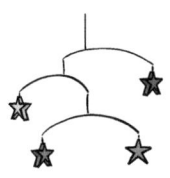

mobile

mòbil per a bressol

board game

joc de taula

dice

daus

model train set

tren elèctric

pacifier

xumet

party

festa

picture book

llibre de dibuixos

ball

pilota

doll

nina

play

jugar

sandpit

sorrera

swing

gronxador

toys

joguines

video game console

consola de jocs de vídeo

tricycle

tricicle

teddy bear

osset de peluix

wardrobe

armari

clothing

roba

socks

mitjons

stockings

mitges

tights

mitja pantaló

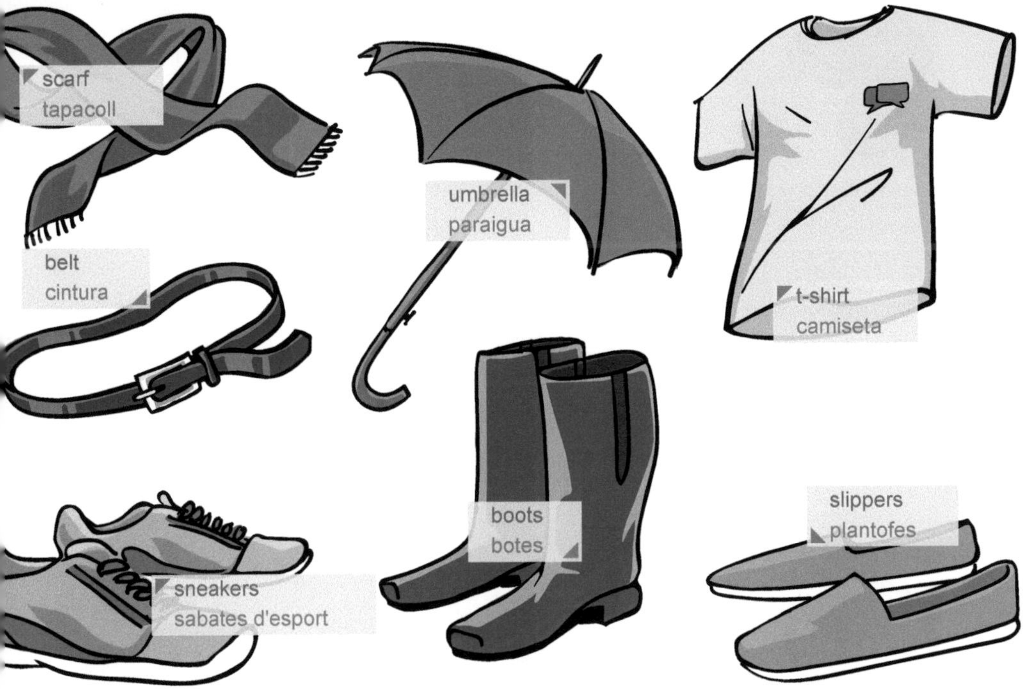

scarf
tapacoll

belt
cintura

umbrella
paraigua

t-shirt
camiseta

sneakers
sabates d'esport

boots
botes

slippers
plantofes

sandals
·················
sandàlies

shoes
·················
sabates

rubber boots
·················
botes de goma

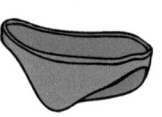

underwear
·················
calçonets

bra
·················
sostenidor

undershirt
·················
guardapits

clothing - roba

body

jjustacòs

pants

pantalons

jeans

jeans

skirt

faldeta

blouse

brusa

shirt

camisa

pullover

jersei

sweater

dessuadora

blazer

blazer

jacket

jaqueta

coat

mantell

raincoat

impermeable

costume

vestit de dona

dress

vestit de dona

wedding dress

vestit de núvia

suit
vestit d'home

nightgown
camisa de dormir

pajamas
pijama

sari
sari

headscarf
mocador de cap

turban
turbant

burka
burca

kaftan
caftan

abaya
abaia

swimsuit
vestit de bany

trunks
calçon(et)s de bany

shorts
pantalons curts

tracksuit
xandall

apron
davantal

gloves
guants

button
botó

glasses
ulleres

bracelet
braçalet

necklace
collaret

ring
anell

earring
orellera

cap
casquet

coat hanger
penjador

hat
capell

tie
corbata

zip
cremallera

helmet
casc

braces
elàstics

school uniform
uniforme escolar

uniform
uniforme

bib

pitet

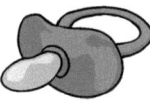

pacifier

xumet

diaper

bolquer

office
oficina

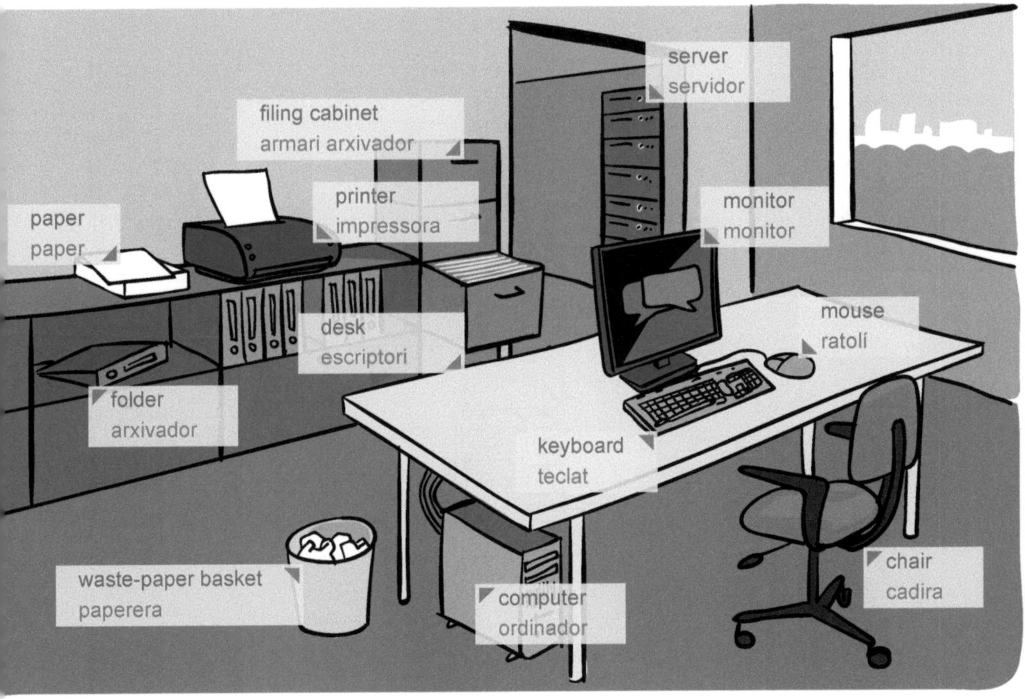

server
servidor

filing cabinet
armari arxivador

printer
impressora

monitor
monitor

paper
paper

mouse
ratolí

desk
escriptori

folder
arxivador

keyboard
teclat

chair
cadira

waste-paper basket
paperera

computer
ordinador

coffee mug

tassa de cafè

calculator

calculadora

internet

Internet

laptop

ordinador portàtil

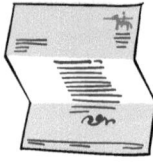

letter

lletra

message

missatge

cell phone

mòbil

network

xarxa

photocopier

fotocopiadora

software

programari

telephone

telèfon

plug socket

presa de corrent

fax machine

fax

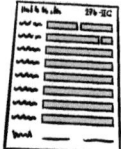

form

formulari

document

document

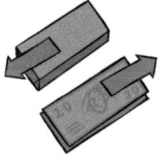

buy

comprar

pay

pagar

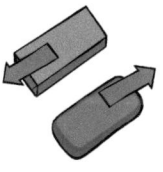

trade

comerciar

money

diners

USD

dollar

dòlar

EUR

euro

euro

JPY

yen

ien

RUB

rouble

ruble

CHF

Swiss franc

franc suís

CNY

renminbi yuan

renminbi

INR

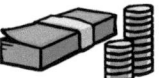

rupee

rupia

cash point

caixa automàtica

currency exchange office

oficina de canvi

gold

or

silver

argent

oil

petroli

energy

energia

price

preu

contract

contracte

tax

impost

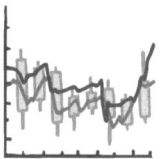

stock

acció

work

treballar

employee

treballador

employer

empresari

factory

fàbrica

shop

botiga

occupations
oficis

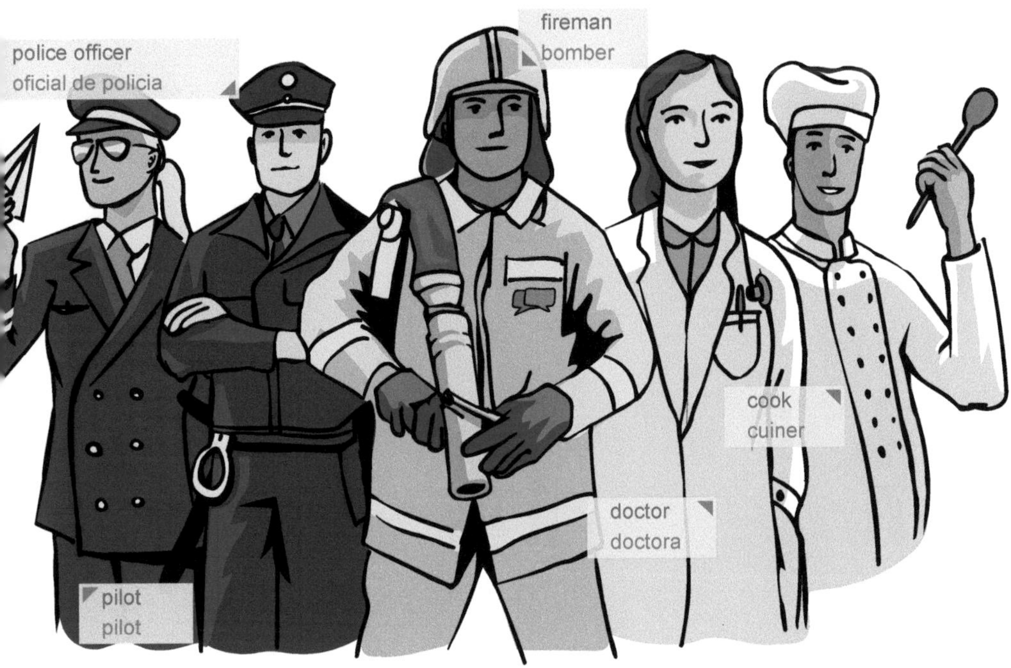

police officer
oficial de policia
fireman
bomber
cook
cuiner
doctor
doctora
pilot
pilot

gardener

jardiner

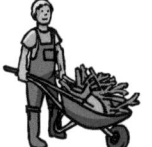

carpenter

fuster

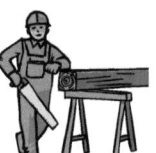

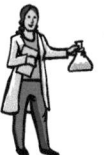

seamstress

costurera

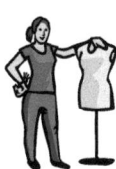

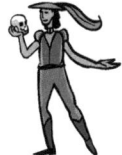

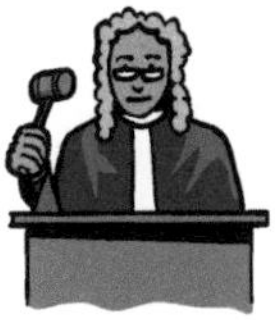

judge

jutge

chemist

química

actor

actor

bus driver

conductor d'autobús

taxi driver

taxista

fisherman

pescador

cleaning lady

dona de la neteja

roofer

ensostrador

waiter

cambrer

hunter

caçador

painter

pintor

baker

forner

electrician

electricista

builder

obrer de la construcció

engineer

enginyer

butcher

carnisser

plumber

llanterner

postman

correu

occupations - oficis

soldier
soldat

architect
arquitecte

cashier
caixera

florist
florista

hairdresser
perruquer

conductor
revisor

mechanic
mecànic

captain
capità

dentist
dentista

scientist
científic

rabbi
rabí

imam
imam

monk
monjo

pastor
capellà

tools
eines

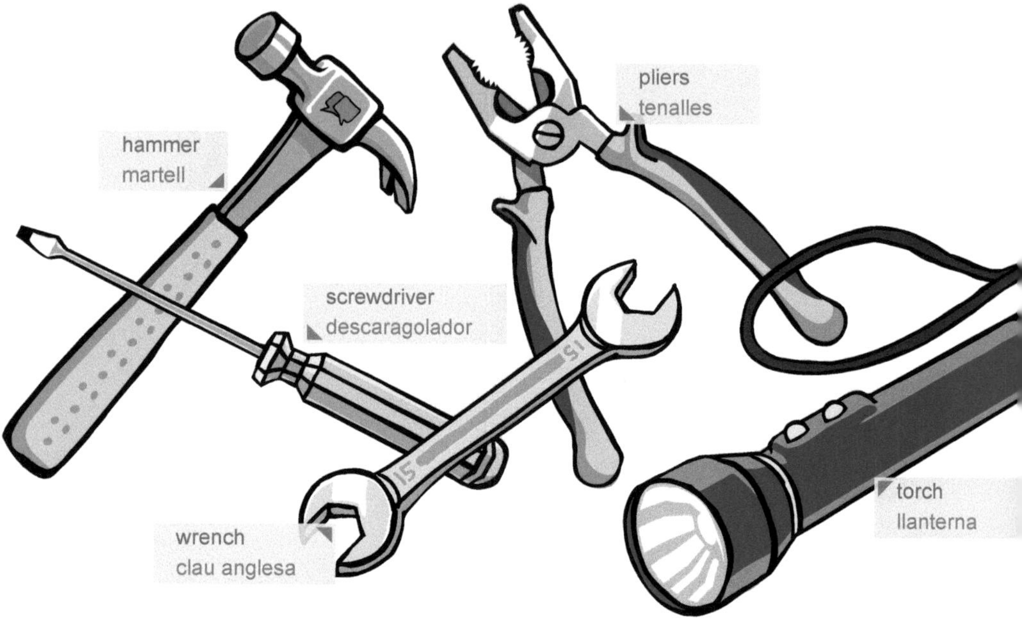
hammer
martell
pliers
tenalles
screwdriver
descaragolador
torch
llanterna
wrench
clau anglesa

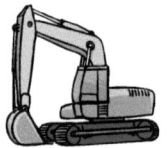

excavator
excavadora

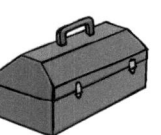

toolbox
caixa d'eines

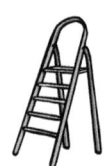

ladder
escala

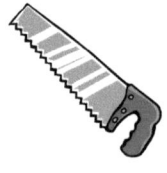

saw
serra

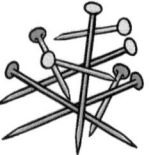

nails
claus

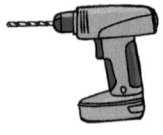

drill
trepant

repair
reparar

shovel
pala

Damn!
Maleït siga!

dustpan
pala

paint can
pot de pintura

screws
caragols

musical instruments
instrument de música

drum set
bateria

loud speaker
altaveu

guitar
guitarra

double bass
contrabaix

trumpet
trompeta

piano

piano

violin

violí

bass

baix

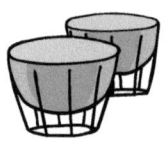

timpani

timbal

drums

tambor

keyboard

teclat

saxophone

saxofon

flute

flauta

microphone

micròfon

ZOO
ZOO

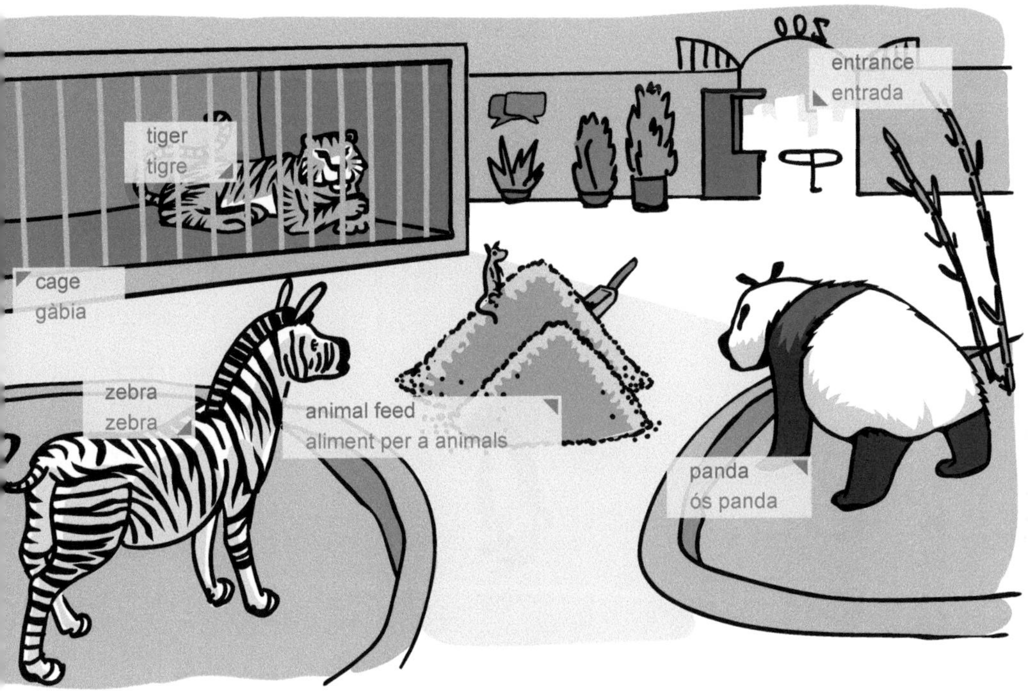
entrance
entrada
tiger
tigre
cage
gàbia
zebra
zebra
animal feed
aliment per a animals
panda
ós panda

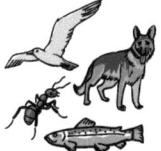

animals
animals

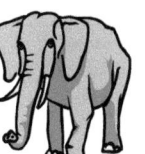

elephant
elefant

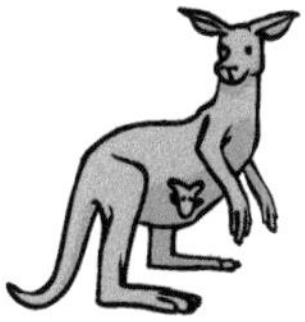

kangaroo
cangurú

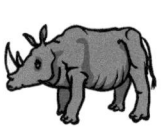

rhino
rinoceront

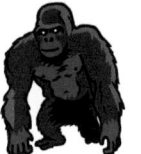

gorilla
goril·la

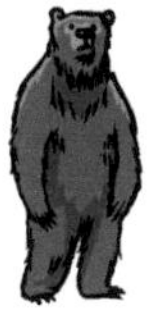

bear
ós

camel

camell

ostrich

estruç

lion

lleó

monkey

simi

flamingo

flamenc

parrot

papagai

polar bear

ós polar

penguin

pingüí

shark

ca mari

peacock

paó

snake

serp

crocodile

cocodril

zookeeper

guardià del zoo

seal

foca

jaguar

jaguar

zoo - zoo

pony
poni

leopard
lleopard

hippo
hipopòtam

giraffe
girafa

eagle
àliga

boar
senglar

fish
peix

turtle
tortuga

walrus
morsa

fox
guineu

gazelle
gasela

American football
futbol americà

cycling
ciclisme

tennis
tenis

basketball
bàsquet

swimming
natació

boxing
boxa

ice hockey
hoquei sobre gel

soccer
futbol americà

badminton
bàdminton

athletics
atletisme

handball
handbol

skiing
esquí

polo
polo

activities
activitats

laugh
riure
jump
saltar
hug
abraçar
walk
anar
sing
cantar
dream
somiar
pray
pregar
kiss
fer un petó

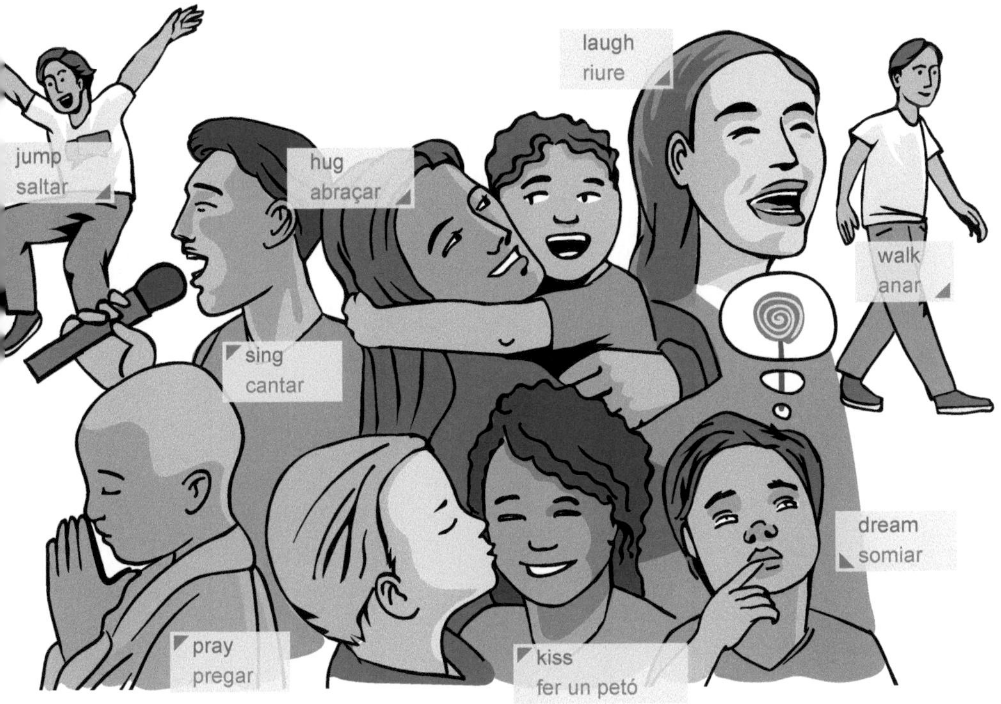

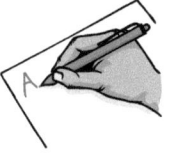

write

escriure

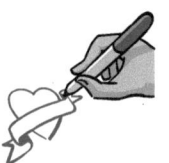

draw

dibuixar

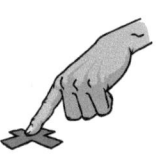

show

mostrar

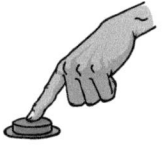

push

pitjar

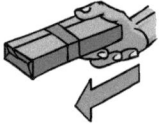

give

donar

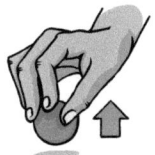

take

prendre

have

tenir

do

fer

be

ésser

stand

estar dret

run

córrer

pull

estirar

throw

llançar

fall

caure

lie

jeure

wait

esperar

carry

portar

sit

asseure's

get dressed

vestir-se

sleep

dormir

wake up

despertar-se

look at

mirar

cry

plorar

stroke

amoixar

comb

pentinar

talk

parlar

understand

comprendre

ask

demanar

listen

escoltar

drink

beure

eat

menjar

tidy up

endreçar

love

estimar

cook

cuinar

drive

conduir

fly

volar

sail

navegar

calculate

calcular

read

llegir

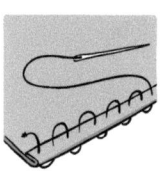

learn

aprendre

work

treballar

marry

casar-se

sew

cosir

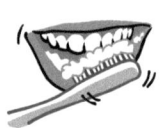

brush teeth

raspallar-se les dents

kill

matar

smoke

fumar

send

enviar

grandmother
via

grandfather
avi

father
pare

mother
mare

baby
nadó

daughter
filla

son
fill

guest

convidat

aunt

tia

uncle

oncle

brother

germà

sister

germana

family - família

body

cos

forehead
front
eye
ull
shoulder
espatlla
finger
dit
face
cara
chin
barbeta
hand
mà
breast
pit
leg
cama
arm
braç

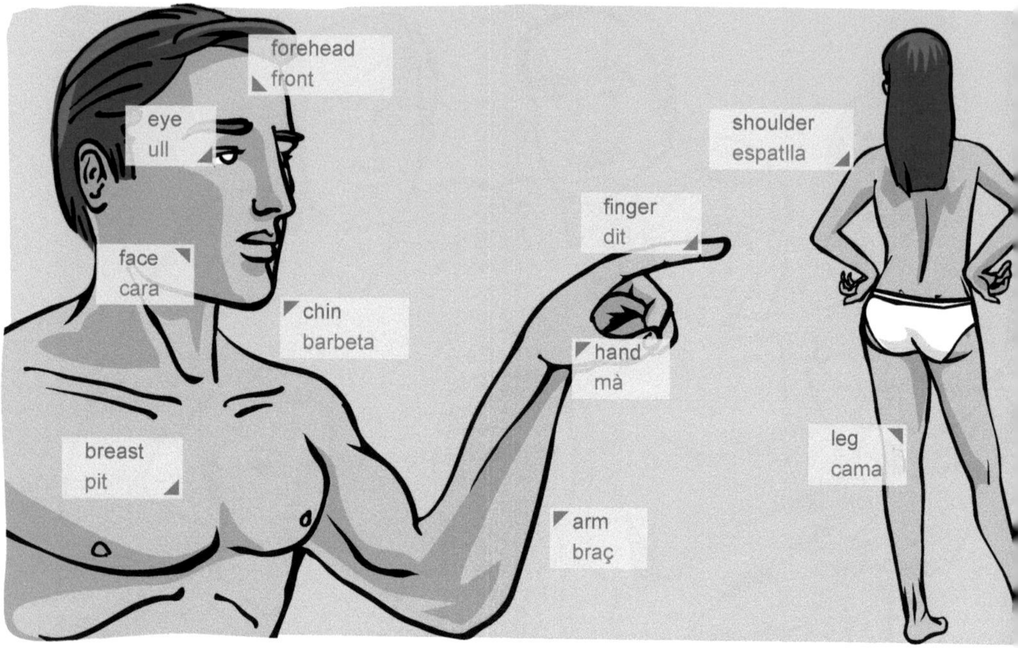

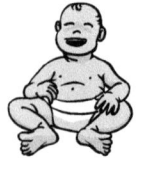

baby

nadó

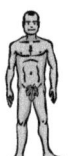

man

home

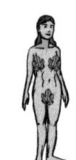

woman

dona

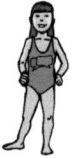

girl

noia

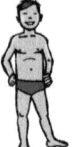

boy

noi

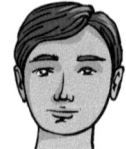

head

cap

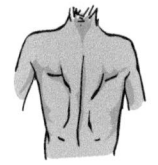	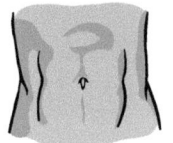	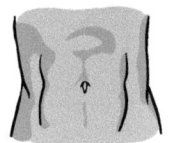
back	belly	navel
esquena	panxa	melic
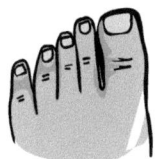	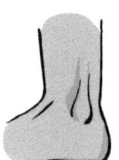	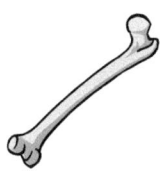
toe	heel	bone
dit gros del peu	taló	os
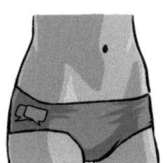	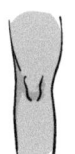	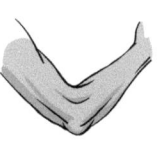
hip	knee	elbow
maluc	genoll	colze
	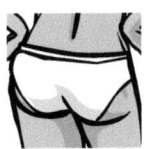	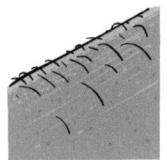
nose	buttocks	skin
nas	cul	pell
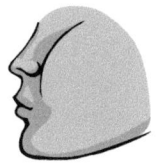	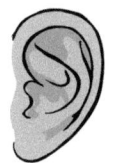	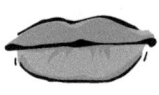
cheek	ear	lip
galta	orella	llavi

mouth

boca

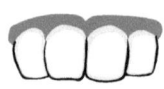

tooth

dent

tongue

llengua

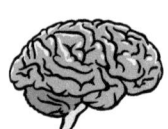

brain

cervell

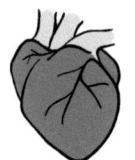

heart

cor

muscle

múscul

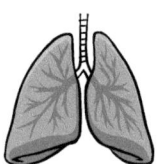

lung

pulmó

liver

fetge

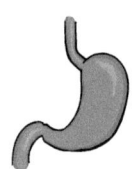

stomach

estómac

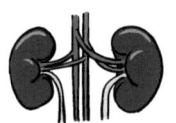

kidneys

ronyó

sex

relació sexual

condom

preservatiu

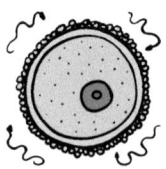

ovum

ovari

semen

semen

pregnancy

prenyat

body - cos

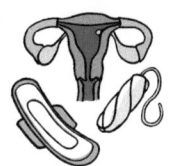

menstruation

menstruació

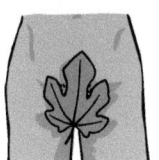

vagina

vagina

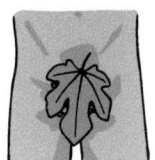

penis

penis

eyebrow

cella

hair

cabells

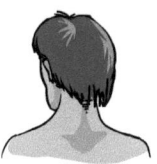

neck

coll

hospital
hospital

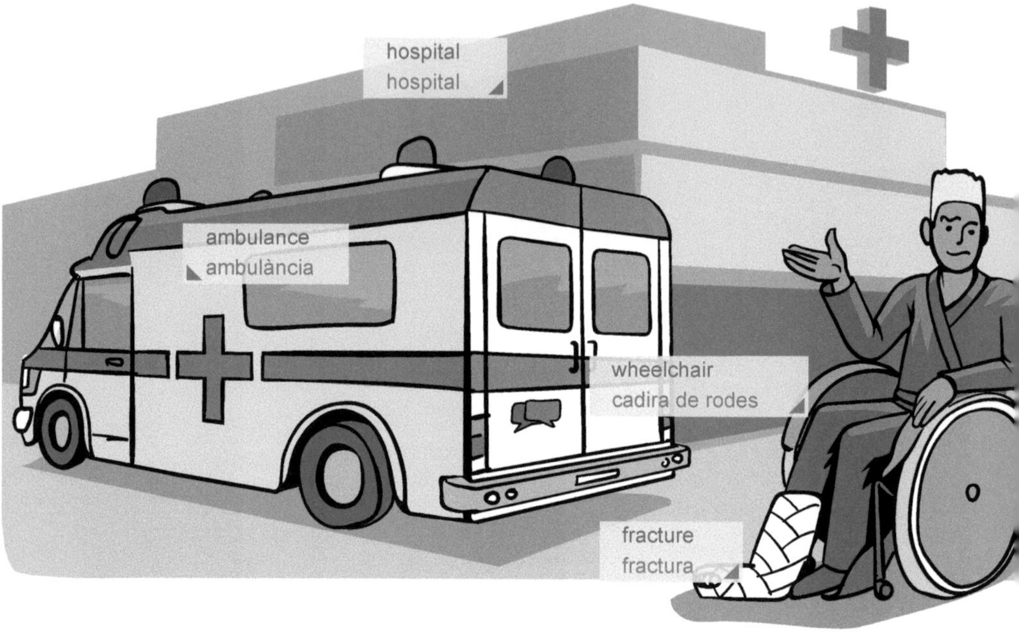

hospital
hospital
ambulance
ambulància
wheelchair
cadira de rodes
fracture
fractura

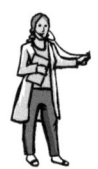

doctor
doctora

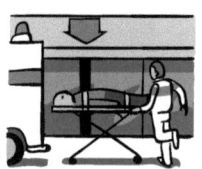

emergency room
sala d'urgències

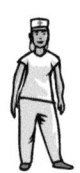

nurse
infermera

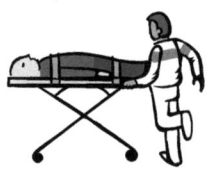

emergency
urgència

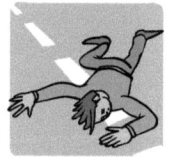

unconscious
inconscient

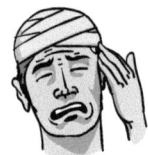

pain
dolor

injury

ferida

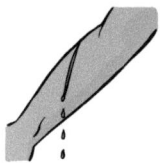

bleeding

sagnament

heart attack

atac de cor

stroke

apoplexia

allergy

al·lèrgia

cough

tos

fever

febre

flu

gripa

diarrhea

diarrea

headache

mal de cap

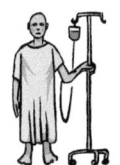

cancer

càncer

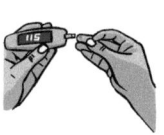

diabetes

diabetis

surgeon

cirurgià

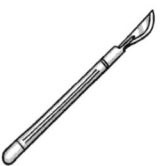

scalpel

escalpel

operation

operació

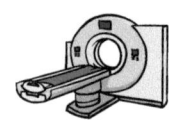

CT

tomografia computada (TC),
TAC

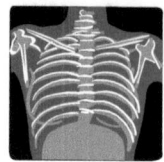

x-ray

raigs x

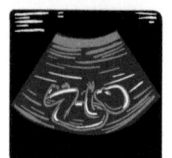

ultrasound

ultrasò

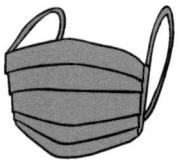

face mask

mascareta

disease

malaltia

waiting room

sala d'espera

crutch

crossa

plaster

tireta

bandage

embenat

injection

injecció

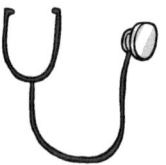

stethoscope

estetoscopi

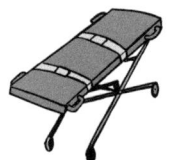

stretcher

llitera

clinical thermometer

termòmetre clínic

birth

pariment

overweight

sobrepès

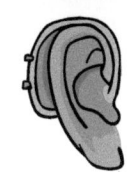

hearing aid

aparell auditiu

disinfectant

desinfectant

infection

infecció

virus

virus

HIV / AIDS

VIH / SIDA

medicine

medicina

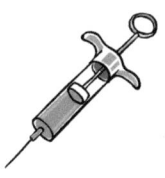

vaccination

vaccí

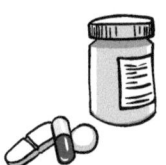

tablets

comprimits

pill

píl·lola

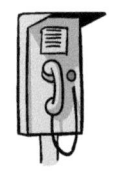

emergency call

trucada d'urgència

blood pressure monitor

tensiòmetre

ill / healthy

malalt / sà

Help!

Socors!

alarm

alarma

assault

assalt

attack

atac

danger

perill

emergency exit

sortida-eixida d'urgència

Fire!

Foc!

fire extinguisher

extintor

accident

accident

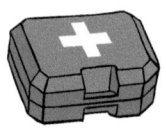

first-aid kit

farmaciola de primers auxilis

SOS

SOS

police

policia

Europe

Europa

North America

Amèrica del Nord

South America

Amèrica del Sud

Africa

Àfrica

Asia

Àsia

Australia

Austràlia

Atlantic

Atlàntic

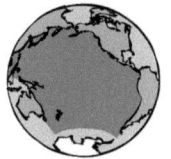

Pacific

Pacífic

Indian Ocean

Oceà Índic

Antarctic Ocean

Oceà Antàrtic

Arctic Ocean

Oceà Àrtic

North pole

pol nord

South pole

pol sud

Antarctica

Antàrtida

earth

terra

land

país

sea

mar

island

illa

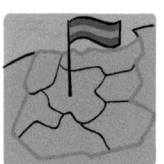

nation

nació

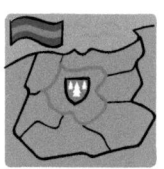

state

estat

clock face

quadrant

hour hand

agulla de les hores

minute hand

agulla dels minuts

second hand

agulla dels segons

What time is it?

Quina hora és?

day

dia

time

temps

now

ara

digital watch

rellotge digital

minute

minut

hour

hora

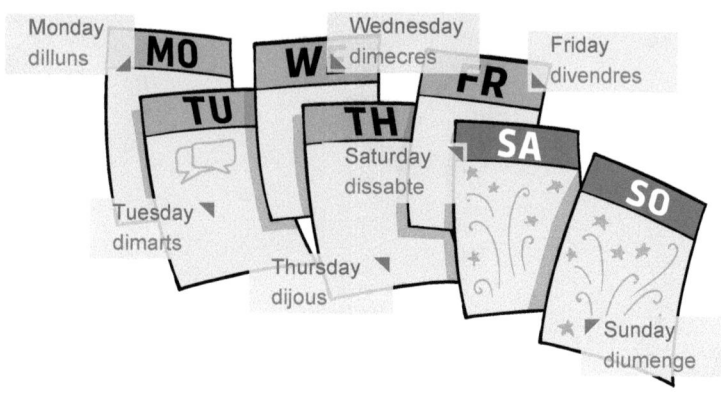

Monday / dilluns
Tuesday / dimarts
Wednesday / dimecres
Thursday / dijous
Friday / divendres
Saturday / dissabte
Sunday / diumenge

yesterday
ahir

today
avui

tomorrow
demà

morning
matí

noon
migdia

evening
tarda

MO	TU	WE	TH	FR	SA	SU
1	2	3	4	5	6	7
8	9	10	11	12	13	14
15	16	17	18	19	20	21
22	23	24	25	26	27	28
29	30	31	1	2	3	4

workdays
dia feiner

MO	TU	WE	TH	FR	SA	SU
1	2	3	4	5	6	7
8	9	10	11	12	13	14
15	16	17	18	19	20	21
22	23	24	25	26	27	28
29	30	31	1	2	3	4

weekend
cap de setmana

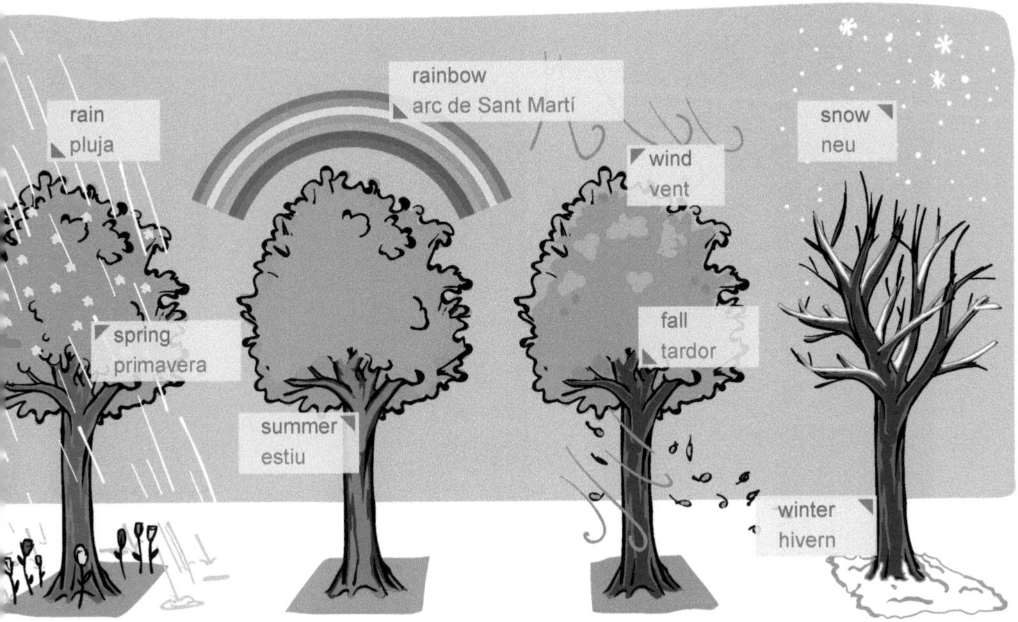

rain
pluja

rainbow
arc de Sant Martí

wind
vent

snow
neu

spring
primavera

summer
estiu

fall
tardor

winter
hivern

4.APRIL	11°	☀
5.APRIL	4°	☁
6.APRIL	13°	☁
7.APRIL	8°	☀
8.APRIL	10°	☀

weather forecast

pronòstic del temps

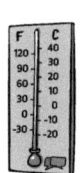

thermometer

termòmetre

sunshine

llum del sol

cloud

núvol

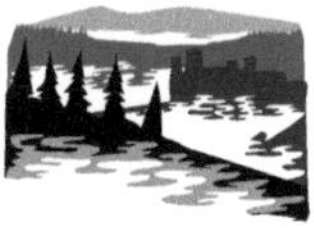

fog

boira

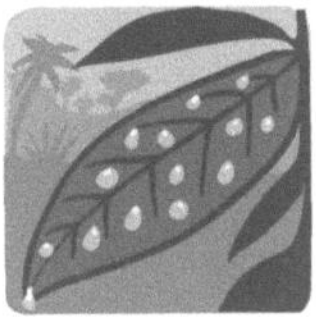

humidity

humiditat de l'aire

lightning

llamp

thunder

tro

storm

tempesta

hail

calamarsa

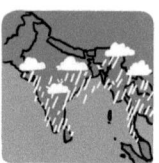

monsoon

monsó

flood

inundació

ice

gel

January

gener

February

febrer

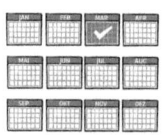

March

març

April

abril

May

maig

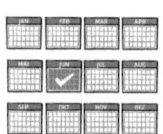

June

juny

July

juliol

August

agost

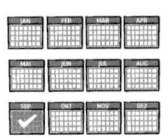

September
....
setembre

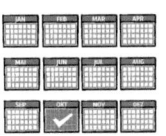

October
....
octubre

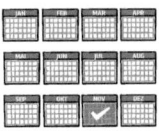

November
....
novembre

December
....
desembre

shapes
formes

circle
....
cercle

square
....
quadrat

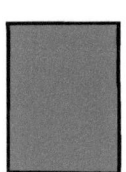

rectangle
....
rectangle

triangle
....
triangle

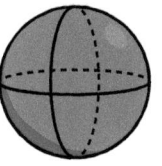

sphere
....
esfera

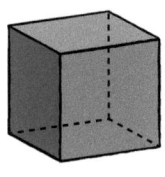

cube
....
cub

white

blanc

yellow

groc

orange

taronja

pink

rosa

red

vermell

purple

lila

blue

blau

green

verd

brown

marró

gray

gris

black

negre

a lot / a little

molt / poc

angry / calm

emprenyat / tranquil

beautiful / ugly

bonic / lleig

beginning / end

començament / fi

big / small

gran / petit

bright / dark

clar / fosc

brother / sister

germà / germana

clean / dirty

net / brut

complete / incomplete

complet / incomplet

day / night

dia / nit

dead / alive

mort / viu

wide / narrow

ample / estret

edible / inedible

comestible / immenjable

evil / kind

dolent / amable

excited / bored

entusiasmat / entediat

fat / thin

gros / prim

first / last

primer / darrer

friend / enemy

amic / enemic

full / empty

ple / buit

hard / soft

dur / tou

heavy / light

pesant / lleuger

hunger / thirst

gana / set

ill / healthy

malalt / sà

illegal / legal

il·legal / legal

intelligent / stupid

intel·ligent / ximple

left / right

esquerra / dreta

near / far

prop / llunyà

new / used
nou / usat

nothing / something
res / quelcom

old / young
vell / jove

on / off
encès / apagat

open / closed
obert / tancat

quiet / loud
silenciós / sorollós

rich / poor
ric / pobre

right / wrong
correcte / incorrecte

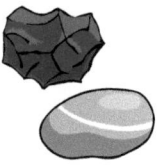

rough / smooth
aspre / suau

sad / happy
trist / content

short / long
curt / llarg

slow / fast
lent / ràpid

wet / dry
humit / sec - eixut

warm / cool
calent / fred

war / peace
guerra / pau

opposites - oposats

0

zero

zero

1

one

u

2

two

dos

3

three

tres

4

four

quatre

5

five

cinc

6

six

sis

7

seven

set

8

eight

vuit

9

nine

nou

10

ten

deu

11

eleven

onze

12

twelve

dotze

13

thirteen

tretze

14

fourteen

catorze

15

fifteen

quinze

16

sixteen

setze

17

seventeen

disset

18

eighteen

divuit

19

nineteen

dinou

20

twenty

vint

100

hundred

cent

1.000

thousand

mil

1.000.000

million

milió

numbers - nombres

languages
llengües

English
....
anglès

American English
....
anglès americà

Chinese Mandarin
....
xinès mandarí

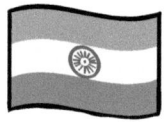

Hindi
....
hindi

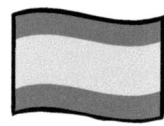

Spanish
....
espanyol

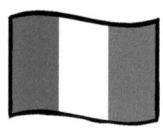

French
....
francès

Arabic
....
àrab

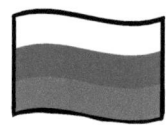

Russian
....
rus

Portuguese
....
portuguès

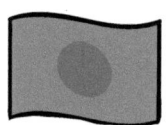

Bengali
....
bengalí

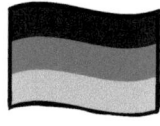

German
....
alemany

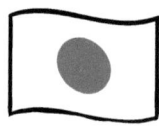

Japanese
....
japonès

I
jo

you
tu

he / she / it
ell / ella / allò

we
nosaltres

you
vosaltres

they
ells

who?
qui?

what?
què?

how?
com?

where?
on?

when?
quan?

name
nom

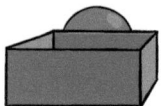

behind

darrere

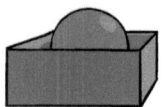

in

en

in front of

davant de

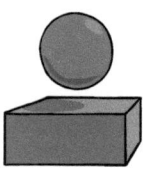

over

damunt

on

sobre

under

sota

beside

al costat

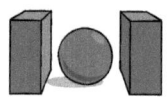

between

entre

place

lloc